D1517728

V is for Virginia

A STATE ALPHABET BOOK

SWEETWATER
PRESS

V is for Virginia
Copyright © 2006 by Sweetwater Press
Produced by Cliff Road Books

ISBN-13: 978-1-58173-526-0
ISBN-10: 1-58173-526-X

All rights reserved. With the exception of brief quotations in critical reviews or articles, no part of this work may be reproduced or transmitted in any form or by any means, electronic or mechanical, including photocopying, recording, or any information storage and retrieval system, without permission in writing from the publisher.

Printed in China

JAMES L. HAMNER PUBLIC LIBRARY

V is for Virginia

E.J. Sullivan

Illustrated by
Ernie Eldredge

SWEETWATER
PRESS

JAMES L. HAMNER PUBLIC LIBRARY
COURT HOUSE, VIRGINIA

920332

A is for apples—we love to eat 'em!

B is for the Blue Ridge in every season.

C is for Chincoteague,
where the ponies run wild.

D is for scenic drives,
mile after mile.

E is for eating everything fried.

F is for founding fathers, who gave us our pride.

G is for George Washington, our first president.

H is for the history that followed where he went

I is for the inns Mom likes, all around us.

J is for John Smith, saved by Pocahontas.

K is for keeping the Hokies team great.

L is for everyone who loves our cool state.

M is for the mountain music we play.

N is for the Navy, down Norfolk way.

O is for over-the-top NASCAR speed.

P is for the Potomac, up by D.C.

Q is for Gramps's quirky stories and jokes.

R is for our relatives in Richmond and Roanoke.

S is for that Shenandoah Valley magic.

T is for the Arlington area traffic.

U is for UV,
go Cavaliers!

V is for Virginia Beach vacations each year.

JAMES L. HAMNER PUBLIC LIBRARY
COURT HOUSE, VIRGINIA

W is for Williamsburg, colonial town.

X marks the Civil War battles of renown.

Y is for Yes! Virginia is the best!

From **Z** back to **A**, it tops all the rest!

FINES
5¢ PER DAY
FOR
OVERDUE BOOKS